A Journey Through
Space

written by Tim de Jongh
illustrated by Jamie O'Brien
edited by Robert Howes, Tim Firth and Pam Goody

The
CHILDREN'S COMPANY Ltd ••• is exactly that
a company formed by friends exclusively for children,
dedicated to providing stimulating material that
both challenges and excites a child's mind

British Library Cataloguing-in-Publication Data. A catalogue record for this
book is available from the British Library.

©1994 International Music Publications Limited
Southend Road, Woodford Green, Essex IG8 8HN, England.

Published by Stave House Publications

STAVE
HOUSE
PUBLICATIONS

Down at the bottom of his garden, behind the potting shed and next to the compost heap, near where the rabbit lived in his hutch, Professor Haffle was building something enormous. It was a tall, pointy, red and silver rocket. Luckily, the Professor had very kind and polite neighbours who were quite used to him making the most extraordinary sorts of things (such as his forty three clockwork cats that instead of 'meeeoow' all said: "Is this your shopping Mrs. Ridlington?"). So they hadn't minded at all when he started to build a rocket out of old washing machines and forty four grandfather clocks.

When it was ready, Professor Haffle went next door and asked Ivan if he wanted to come for a trip up into space after tea. "Yes please!" said Ivan who was great friends with the Professor. So the Professor packed the rocket with all the things they would need for the journey, such as scones, tea and a camera. Most important of all was a large map of all the planets nearby. These are The Sun, Mercury, Venus, Mars, Jupiter, Saturn, Uranus, Neptune and Pluto. The Professor had drawn them all on a large table cloth.

At last they were all set. The Professor pressed lots of buttons, and all kinds of lights came on. There was a strange fizzing sound, clicking things clocked and clicked.

A grandfather clock struck eighty two and the rocket took off. Ivan looked out of the window and saw the houses vanish below. Hundreds of dials squeaked. The engines roared. "Look at our speed!" cried the Professor. "We're doing 28,000 kilometres an hour!"

As it happens space rockets have to go at least 28,000 kilometres an hour or they'd never get away from the Earth. This is because of something called gravity. Gravity is the force that makes everything stick to our planet and not float off into the sky.

Soon the rocket had left the Earth behind and a big orange light came on and flashed. It said "Fire the first stage!" The Professor took hold of a great big lever and pulled with all his might. There was a swooshing sound and a large part of the rocket fell off the back towards the Earth. "Yippee!" cried the Professor. "It works." Most rockets that go up into space are really made up of three rockets joined together, one on top of the other. Each of these small rockets has its own engine and fuel tank. When the fuel in one is all used up it is dropped off into space where it catches fire and burns up like a gigantic firework. The professor had just fired the first stage from his rocket.

Soon the Professor, and Ivan were in space above the Earth. One of the Professor's clockwork cats had sneaked on board. "Is this your shopping Mrs. Ridlington?" it said to the Professor as he stroked it. Ivan looked out of the window and saw the clouds over the Earth swirling below them. All about were satellites gleaming in the sunlight as they circled the Earth. There were also lots of bits of old rockets and space things nobody wanted any more floating about. This is called space debris. The satellites did lots of different jobs. Some bounced TV pictures around the Earth, some helped with telephone calls, some took pictures of the Earth to show what kind of weather was expected.

After the Professor had fired the next stage, he made a cup of tea and all was quiet and still as the rocket glided slowly through the thick blackness. "Where are we going?" asked Ivan. The Professor spread out his table cloth with the drawings of all the nearby planets on it. "This is our solar system!" he said. "The Earth circles the Sun, all the time spinning round, and there are several other planets that also circle our Sun. They are called Mercury, Venus, Mars, Jupiter, Saturn, Uranus, Neptune and Pluto. This is our solar system." The Professor was quite right about this, because he was nearly always quite right about everything. (Except the time he invented a golf ball that could shout so you knew where it was because it had gone completely wrong and started shouting just as you were about to hit it.)

Our solar system

The Sun

Mercury 88 days

Venus 225 days

Earth 365 days

Mars 780 days

Jupiter 12 years

Saturn 29 years

Uranus 84 years

Neptune 165 years

Pluto 248 years

"How about a trip to Pluto?" said the Professor, pointing with a piece of toast to the furthest planet in the solar system. "Pluto!" said Ivan. "Fantastic!" And the Professor began to do some very complicated sums on his white coat. As it happens Pluto is an enormously long way away from the Earth and it would take a red bus about ten thousand years to get there. "Good thing this isn't a normal rocket!" muttered the Professor. Normal rockets work like this: their fuel tanks are full of nitrogen and oxygen. When these two things are mixed together they explode out the back of the rocket. This pushes it forwards. The same sort of thing happens if you blow up a balloon and let go of it. The air whizzes out the back which makes the balloon go forwards. But the Professor's wasn't a normal rocket at all.

Incase of an emergency break glass... Prof. Haffle

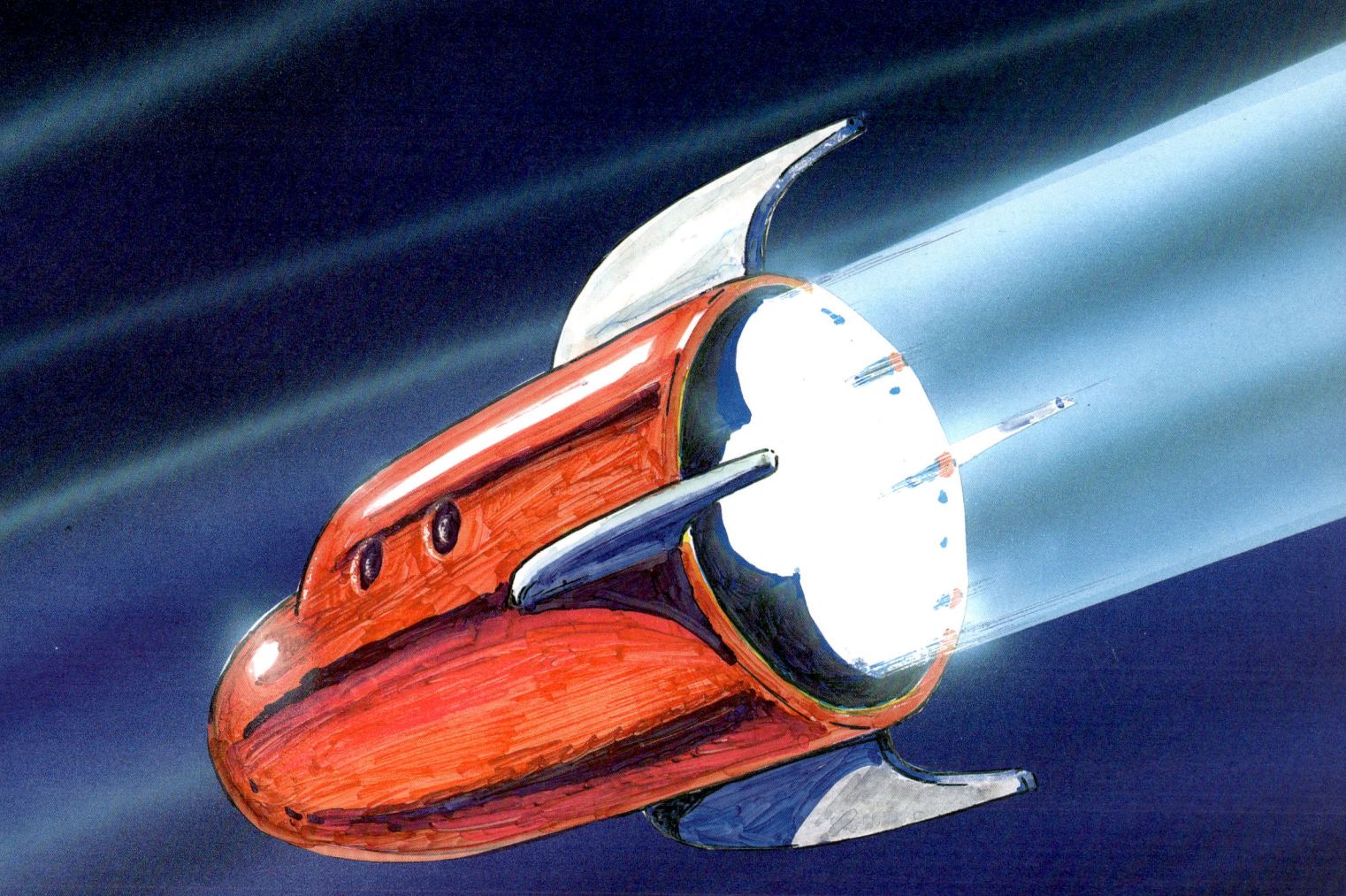

The Professor finished working out a very complicated sum on his right arm and cried, "I'm going to have to go to warp speed!" Then he pulled no end of levers, and pressed banks of large green buttons.

There was a whizzing humming noise, a grandfather clock struck forty six and a half, and the rocket shook and roared forwards faster than the speed of light. This was very clever indeed. Not even the rockets made by very clever scientists in America and Russia could go as fast as this. Everything whizzed by.

Then all the shaking stopped and the rocket came to a neat stop just outside the planet of Pluto. "Excellent!" said the Professor. "There she is." The planet swirled about below the rocket as Ivan looked out of the tiny window. What they had done was really quite impossible because nothing goes faster than light which can travel at 300,000 kilometres in just one second. In fact, it would take a car travelling day and night for four months without any traffic jams to also cover 300,000 kilometres. But the Professor was quite used to doing things that were impossible. "Pluto is very different from all the other planets in our solar system" he said. "It is very small — only about half the size of earth, and it is also a very long way away from the Sun. It takes Pluto two hundred and forty eight years to do just one circle around the Sun!" The Professor sat back and gazed into the blackness of the Universe which went on and on. "Right!" he said at last (having suddenly thought of an idea for a backwards alarm clock that instead of waking you up would send you to sleep). "Let's get going!"

The next planet the Professor and Ivan stopped at was Neptune. It was a beautiful blue planet made mostly out of gas. "Four times larger than the Earth" said the Professor as they pressed their noses against the window. "One of Neptune's moons, Triton, is the coldest place in our solar system. The temperature goes down to minus two hundred and thirty five degrees centigrade!"

"Brrrr!" said Ivan.

"At that temperature a lettuce leaf would freeze so hard you could use it as a hammer. On to Uranus now or we'll never get back for your bed time," said the Professor.

After pushing a lot more buttons that all went ping! they reached Uranus. Uranus was also made mostly out of gas. And it circles the sun on it's side as though it had fallen over. "Fantastic isn't it?" said the Professor.

"Yes", said Ivan. "How many planets are there like this in the whole universe?"

"Millions and millions and millions and millions" said the Professor. Ivan stared down at Uranus trying to imagine all these other planets spinning around in space. "Right — come on, next planet!" said the Professor pushing a large blue handle that made steam come out of a washing machine and the hands on a grandfather clock spin round. The Professor's rocket roared past the thick black rings. The rings on Uranus are some of the blackest material in our solar system. Even blacker than when the Professor burnt his toast. So that just goes to show how enormously black they are.

The rocket zigged and zagged and then stopped by the planet Saturn. This planet had rings around it too. But these ones were made mostly out of big chunks of ice. The Professor gently glided the rocket up to them. Some of them were as big as a house. In the distance Ivan could see many of the moons of Saturn spinning around among all the ice. "Saturn has no end of moons" said the Professor. "It's got more moons than I've had bananas today." The Professor ate lots of bananas, so Ivan knew this had to be a lot of moons. "How many?" he asked.

"Eighteen!" said the Professor. "Atlas, Pandora, Prometheus, Atlas, Janus, Epimetheus, Mimas, Enceladus, Calypso, Telesto, Tethys, Helene, Dione, Rhea, Titan, Hyperion, Iapetus, Phoebe." And he suddenly had eighteen new ideas of names for his clockwork cats. "We shall call you Mimas!" said the Professor, stroking the clockwork cat which had sneaked on board.

"Is this your shopping Mrs. Ridlington?" it purred.

"Right! Jupiter! The biggest planet in our solar system" said the Professor as they arrived. "I think this is a good spot to take a picture for your scrap-book". And he got out a complicated special camera he had invented. This camera was so clever it could tell you where the best place was to stand. "A bit to the left!" growled the camera. "No not that far!" it added, as it wasn't feeling too well. Behind them was Jupiter, a big, stormy world mostly made of gas. The biggest planet in our solar system by quite a long way. It had sixteen moons and a very faint ring. It also had a great red spot near the middle which was a giant storm that had been going on for at least three hundred years.

"That's it!" said the camera, and took a picture. Then it took another. Then it took six at once and began making a nasty "grrrrrrrrrrr" noise and started smoking. "Look out!" said the Professor hitting it with a frying pan. There was a nasty "Smile pleeeeeeeease!" and the camera shot up to the ceiling, knocked no end of buttons, and exploded in a ball of white light.

"Interesting" said the Professor as the rocket shot off into space.

"That's Mars!" shouted the Professor, pressing seventeen buttons and setting a grandfather clock at ten to three. But the rocket had no interest in stopping at all. In fact it seemed to be going faster and faster. Ivan clung on as they rocketed past Mars with hardly time to blink. He just saw it. A small solid red planet with mountains, deserts and ice caps. (People once said there might be life on Mars, but scientists sent a small space craft there and found there wasn't any. So if you meet a Martian in the street make sure you ask to see some identification. Because the chances are, it's just your next door neighbour wrapped up in tin foil.)

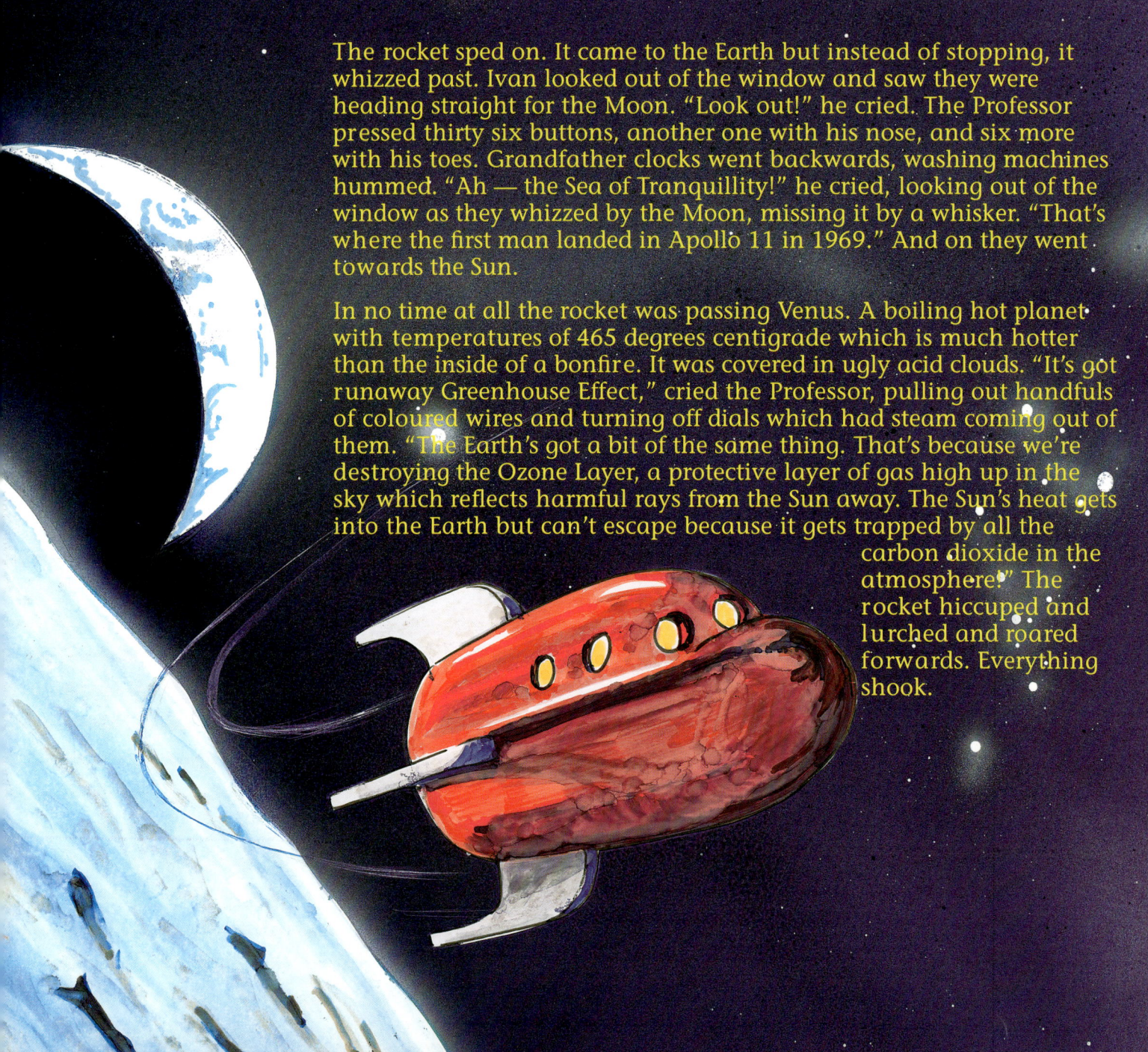

The rocket sped on. It came to the Earth but instead of stopping, it whizzed past. Ivan looked out of the window and saw they were heading straight for the Moon. "Look out!" he cried. The Professor pressed thirty six buttons, another one with his nose, and six more with his toes. Grandfather clocks went backwards, washing machines hummed. "Ah — the Sea of Tranquillity!" he cried, looking out of the window as they whizzed by the Moon, missing it by a whisker. "That's where the first man landed in Apollo 11 in 1969." And on they went towards the Sun.

In no time at all the rocket was passing Venus. A boiling hot planet with temperatures of 465 degrees centigrade which is much hotter than the inside of a bonfire. It was covered in ugly acid clouds. "It's got runaway Greenhouse Effect," cried the Professor, pulling out handfuls of coloured wires and turning off dials which had steam coming out of them. "The Earth's got a bit of the same thing. That's because we're destroying the Ozone Layer, a protective layer of gas high up in the sky which reflects harmful rays from the Sun away. The Sun's heat gets into the Earth but can't escape because it gets trapped by all the carbon dioxide in the atmosphere!" The rocket hiccuped and lurched and roared forwards. Everything shook.

"Mercury!" shouted the Professor as they streaked by. "The last planet before the Sun". Ivan just saw it for a moment out of the window. "It goes round the Sun once every eighty eight days!" he cried. The Professor was very clever at remembering things like this, though he was not very good at remembering how to stop his rocket when it was zooming towards the great big ball of fire that was the Sun. He tried all kinds of buttons, levers and handles. He tried pushing things, pulling things, turning things, and hitting other things with a saucepan. Grandfather clocks, clocked and clicked, struck half past six hundred and nine and then whizzed backwards until they exploded. Washing machines hummed and growled. But the rocket didn't want to stop. It zigged and zagged and roared forwards.

The rocket sped towards the very centre of the Sun.

"What's going to happen?" shouted Ivan.

"Well, I could try upside downing, the upside down, right-way-up, upside-down, right-way-up o'meter," said the Professor, doing quite the most complicated sum possible that went right down the back of his white coat and up the other side. In front of the rocket the Sun boiled and frothed. It was the largest thing they had ever seen. A massive glowing and throbbing star four times bigger than all the planets they had seen put together. Stars are very heavy planets with a giant burning core which is pressed inwards by heavy outer layers. These outer layers stop the burning getting out of control. Our Sun has been burning like a gigantic hydrogen bomb for five billion years.

Suddenly the rocket was still. Everything inside was quiet and calm as they hung silently in space. "Well, that was all very much of a something" said the Professor, rather out of breath, coming out from inside a grandfather clock holding handfuls of wires. He looked about the rocket, which needed a lot of tidying up.

"Meeeow!" said Mimas. "Meow?" repeated the Professor. "Meeeeeeow" said Mimas.

Ivan picked up the clockwork cat. "I've stopped the rocket" said the Professor, "and mended the cat all in one go. It must have been the hu-jimmy-whatsit-thingumy. Time for home?"

"Yes" said Ivan. The Professor and Ivan each ate an emergency banana, from a special red glass case the Professor had on the wall. And then the Professor set the rocket for the Earth.

". . . . four, three, two, one, splashdown!" cried the Professor, as the rocket landed with a jolt. "Well that's funny" he said looking out of the window. "I don't recognise this at all. Most odd."

"It's all right Professor" said Ivan looking out of the window. "We've landed in the penguin enclosure of London Zoo." Ivan and the Professor had the most awful time explaining to the Zoo Keeper what they were doing there. It wasn't until the Professor agreed to invent a machine, that would throw fish into the air for the penguins three times a day all by itself, that the Zoo Keeper calmed down.

It was already dark when the taxi arrived to take them home. The taxi driver was very surprised to be asked to tow the Professor's rocket, but in the end he agreed. As they began their journey through the town Ivan gazed out of the back window at the stars. "And that" said the Professor, spreading out the table cloth, "was just our solar system. There are millions and millions of other solar systems in our bit of space. They all go together to make our galaxy. And our galaxy is called The Milky Way."

The taxi driver pulled up outside the Professor's house. "Meeeow!" said Mimas, the clockwork cat to all the other clockwork cats that were waiting for them.

"Is that your shopping Mrs. Ridlington?" they all purred together. Ivan and the taxi driver helped the Professor push his rocket down to the bottom of his garden in the moonlight. "And our galaxy," he puffed, "is just one tiny galaxy among millions and millions and millions and billions of other galaxies in the Universe. If the Universe was the size of a vast ocean, the Earth wouldn't even be as big as one egg cup full of water".

And Ivan looked up into the sky at all the specks of light and tried to imagine all the stars and all the planets in all the galaxies in the Universe swirling and swishing about in the treacle thick darkness of space.